ARCTIC FOXES POUNCE, LEMMINGS BURROW

HUNTER AND HUNTED
ANIMAL SURVIVAL

MICHAELA SEYMOUR

PowerKiDS press.
New York

Published in 2018 by The Rosen Publishing Group, Inc.
29 East 21st Street, New York, NY 10010

First Edition

Editor: Theresa Morlock
Book Design: Reann Nye

Photo Credits: Cover (Arctic fox) Vladimir Melnik/Shutterstock.com; cover (lemming), p. 1 Westend61/Getty Images; p. 4 moosehenderson/Shutterstock.com; p. 5 Peter Hermes Furian/Shutterstock.com; pp. 6, 17 TOM MCHUGH/Science Source/Getty Images; p. 7 Martin Hejzlar/Shutterstock.com; p. 8 Eric Baccega/Nature Picture Library/Getty Images; p. 9 (lemming) Karelian/Shutterstock.com; p. 9 (mouse) Rudmer Zwerver/Shutterstock.com; p. 9 (groundhog) Rabbitti/Shutterstock.com; pp. 10, 22 (lemming) Sven-Erik Arndt/Picture Press/Getty Images; p. 11 BMJ/Shutterstock.com; p. 12 Menno Schaefer/Shutterstock.com; p. 13 Anders Peter Photography/Shutterstock.com; p. 14 Theo Allofs/Photodisc/Getty Images; p. 15 Incredible Arctic/Shutterstock.com; p. 16 Enn Li Photography/Moment/Getty Images;p. 18 Steven Kazlowski/Science Faction/Getty Images; p. 19 Roine Magnusson/The Image Bank/Getty Images; p. 20 Ton Koene photography/Moment/Getty Images; p. 21 Kris Grabiec/Shutterstock.com; p. 22 (arctic fox) NaturesMomentsuk/Shutterstock.com.

Cataloging-in-Publication Data

Names: Seymour, Michaela.
Title: Arctic foxes pounce, lemmings burrow / Michaela Seymour.
Description: New York : PowerKids Press, 2018. | Series: Hunter and hunted: animal survival | Includes index.
Identifiers: ISBN 9781508156727 (pbk.) | ISBN 9781508156666 (library bound) | ISBN 9781508156550 (6 pack)
Subjects: LCSH: Arctic fox–Juvenile literature. | Lemmings–Juvenile literature.
Classification: LCC QL737.C22 S49 2018 | DDC 599.776'4–dc23

Manufactured in the United States of America

CPSIA Compliance Information: Batch Batch #BS17PK: For Further Information contact Rosen Publishing, New York, New York at 1-800-237-9932

CONTENTS

LIFE IN THE ARCTIC CIRCLE

The Arctic Circle surrounds the North Pole, the northernmost point on the planet. It's made up of the Arctic Ocean and parts of the continents around it. Much of the land in the Arctic Circle is tundra, a very cold habitat with no trees and frozen ground. During winter, **temperatures** drop below -40° Fahrenheit (-40° Celsius).

This icy place isn't easy to live in, but **species** such as Arctic foxes and lemmings call it home. These creatures have **adapted** to survive in the harsh Arctic **climate**.

WILDLIFE WISDOM

The word "arctic" comes from the Greek word *arktos*, which means "bear." The Arctic got its name from Ursa Minor and Ursa Major, which are bear-shaped constellations, or groups of stars, in the northern sky.

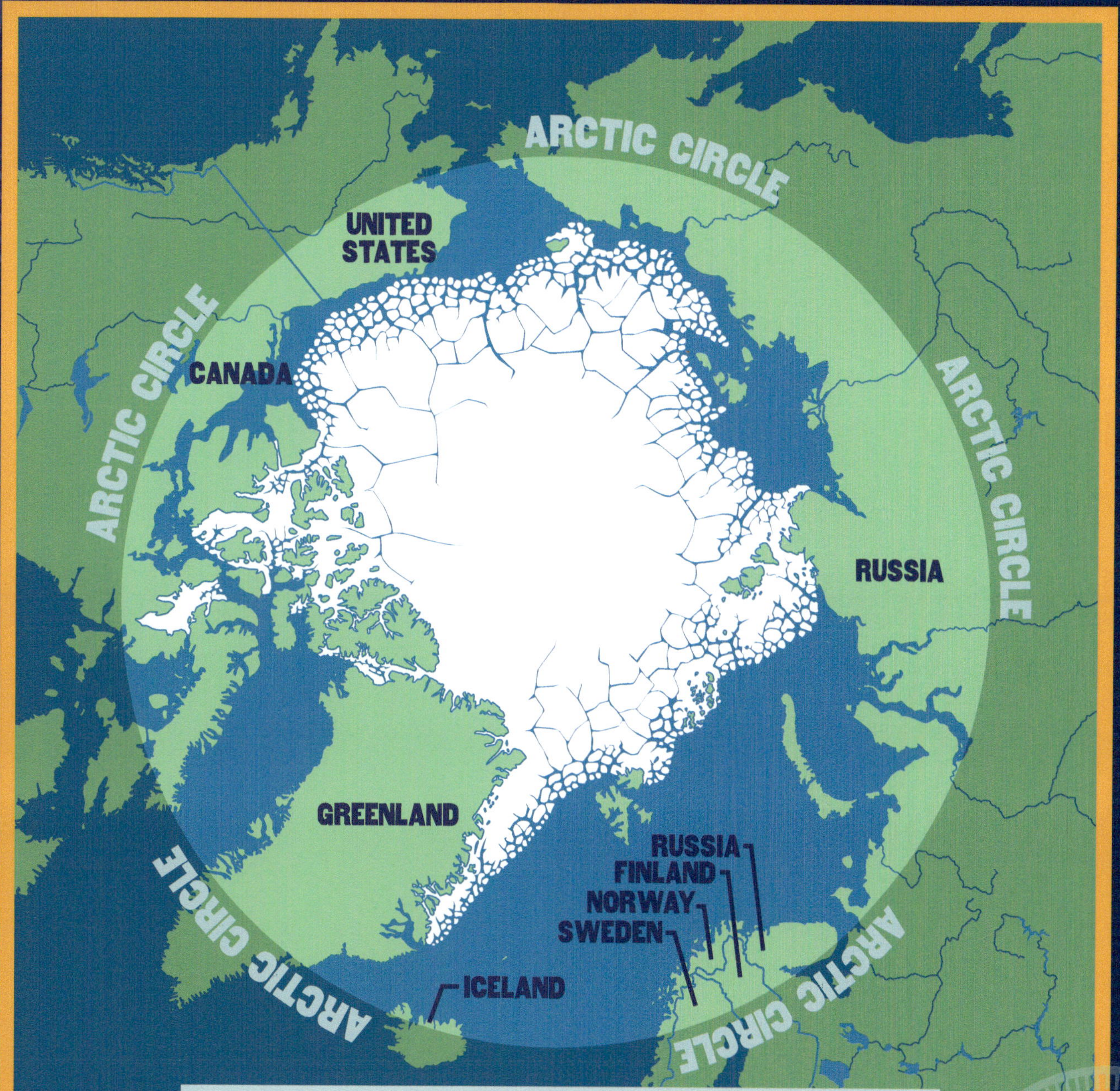

Parts of the United States, Canada, Finland, Greenland, Iceland, Norway, Sweden, and Russia are all in the Arctic.

LITTLE LEMMINGS

There are about 20 different species of lemmings in the Arctic. They range from about 3 to 6 inches (8 to 15 cm) long and weigh between 1 to 4 ounces (28 to 113 g).

Lemmings have small, sturdy bodies with short legs. They have tiny ears, beady black eyes, and a stubby tail. Their small body makes it easier for lemmings to stay warm in low temperatures. They also have a thick coat of soft fur to keep out the cold. During the summer, their fur is brown or gray. In the winter, it's white.

In the wild, lemmings only live for one to three years.

Lemmings are herbivores, which means they eat plants but not meat. In the tundra, plants are mostly grasses, herbs, mosses, and shrubs. Luckily, lemmings are not picky eaters. They'll even eat roots and twigs!

Lemmings use their sharp teeth and claws to dig burrows in the hard ground. A burrow is an underground tunnel where an animal makes its home. Some lemmings live in groups, but some only come together to **mate** and **migrate**.

HAMSTER IN BURROW

Lemmings are rodents, which are mammals with ever-growing front teeth. Mice, hamsters, and groundhogs are also rodents.

POPULATION FLUX

Female lemmings have litters of up to 13 babies multiple times each year. If they're not kept in check by predators, lemming populations can rise extremely high. Groups then migrate to seek new food sources.

The lemming population has a huge effect on other species. Lemmings are the main prey of Arctic foxes. When lemming populations rise, so do fox populations. When they drop, fox populations drop too. These population cycles show how much animals rely on each other in an **ecosystem**. This is especially true in the tundra, where there is less **biodiversity**.

WILDLIFE WISDOM

In 1958, a Disney nature documentary called *White Wilderness* spread the **myth** that lemmings kill themselves by jumping off cliffs into the ocean. This is false. Lemmings are very good swimmers and sometimes try to cross bodies of water to a new home. However, sometimes they will drown if the body of water is too large.

When lemming populations drop, Arctic foxes have few other sources of food. This limited food supply is why population spikes and dips can be much larger or smaller in the tundra than in other parts of the world.

FEISTY FOXES

Arctic foxes are about 2 feet (0.6 m) long and about 9 inches (22.9 cm) tall. Their bushy tail can be 12 inches (30.5 cm) long! A fox's tail helps it balance and gives it a warm covering to snuggle under at night.

Arctic foxes have layered fur that's brown or gray in the summer and white in the winter. Their paws are covered in fur to protect them from ice and snow. Foxes live in underground dens, often reusing dens built by other foxes. Some dens are hundreds of years old.

Arctic foxes are the only native land mammal in Iceland.

Foxes mate for life. Males and females pair up in the spring and have litters of up to 14 pups—that's one of the largest litters of any wild mammal! Fox parents raise their young in the den. The mother cares for the pups while the father goes out to look for food.

A female fox is called a vixen.

WILDLIFE WISDOM

Polar bears are the apex predator of the Arctic ecosystem. That means that no other predators hunt them, and they are at the top of the food chain. Polar bears rely on sea ice to travel and hunt. As sea ice melts from **global warming**, polar bears are at risk of starving.

Although lemmings are their favorite food, foxes are willing to eat almost anything. Sometimes they'll follow polar bears or wolves, waiting to **scavenge** their leftovers. Foxes even store food within cold parts of their dens, which act like refrigerators.

FIERCE SURVIVORS

Lemmings and Arctic foxes have adaptations that prepare them for life in the Arctic. Both animals have **compact** bodies that help keep them warm. Both have fur that changes colors with the seasons to blend in with their surroundings. Both build underground homes to avoid predators and the cold.

WILDLIFE WISDOM

Camouflage is an adaptation that allows an animal to blend in with its surroundings. Many animals in the Arctic are white to blend in with the surrounding snow and ice. Other animals change color as they grow up or shed their fur with the seasons.

Lemmings may be small, but they are survivors!

These animals can endure extremely cold temperatures, high winds that blow up to 60 miles (96.6 km) per hour, and a scarce food supply. But what happens when lemmings and foxes are pitted against each other in the battle for survival?

FACE-OFF!

Foxes use their sharp hearing to find lemmings burrowing beneath the snow. Foxes tip their ears toward the ground, listening for the scamper of a lemming. Then they rear up on their hind legs and pounce! They dive headfirst into the snow, breaking into the lemming's burrow.

However, lemmings are very good at hiding their burrows. Burrows are built under several feet of snow. Foxes can sometimes get stuck in the snow when they dive down to attack. Lemmings use their sharp claws to help them scramble away from attacking foxes. As a last defense, they use their sharp teeth to bite and scare a predator away.

In this matchup, it's clear Arctic foxes often catch lemmings for a meal. However, lemmings reproduce so quickly they have huge populations.

KEEPING THE BALANCE

Though they're predators and prey, Arctic foxes and lemmings need each other to survive. Foxes need lemmings for food. Lemmings need foxes to keep their populations in control. Each species has a set of skills and adaptations that help it survive. Foxes can't always catch lemmings, and lemmings can't always escape foxes. That way, the ecosystem stays in balance.

Unfortunately, human activities have upset this natural balance. Global warming is changing the climate of the Arctic, and as temperatures rise, sea ice melts. Rising temperatures affect every plant and animal in an ecosystem.

This fox is caught in a metal trap from which it can't escape. Arctic foxes are targeted by hunters who trap and kill them to sell their fur. This can disrupt the balance in the tundra.

WILDLIFE WISDOM

Arctic sea ice reflects about 80 percent of the sunlight that hits it. As global temperatures rise, sea ice melts, causing the ocean to soak up more sunlight and become warmer. Because all oceans are connected, the temperature of the Arctic Ocean affects the climate everywhere.

TEAM FOX VS. TEAM LEMMING

The species that call the frozen tundra home face a never-ending struggle to find food, avoid predators, and stay warm. In the Arctic Circle, only the toughest and the cleverest can hope to survive.

Though they share many strengths, the Arctic fox and lemming are natural enemies. Thinking about their amazing abilities, it's not easy to decide which to root for in the final battle of life or death. Who would you choose? The fierce pouncing fox or the burrowing lemming?

GLOSSARY

adapt: To change in order to live better in a certain environment.

biodiversity: The number of different species living in an area.

climate: The average weather conditions in an area over a period of time.

compact: Using little space.

ecosystem: A natural community of living and nonliving things.

global warming: A gradual increase in Earth's temperatures. It is believed to be caused by gases that are released when people burn fossil fuels such as gasoline.

mate: One of two animals that come together to make babies, or to come together to make babies.

migrate: To move from one area to another for feeding or having babies.

myth: A story believed by many people that is not true.

scavenge: To search for food to eat.

species: A group of plants or animals that are all the same kind.

temperature: How hot or cold something is.

INDEX

WEBSITES

Due to the changing nature of Internet links, PowerKids Press has developed an online list of websites related to the subject of this book. This site is updated regularly. Please use this link to access the list: www.powerkidslinks.com/handh/fox